THIS BOOK BELONGS TO:

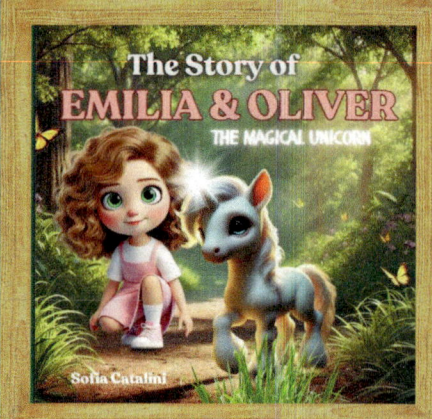

OTHER BOOKS you may like

Scan QR or Visit Website
WWW.IGESCABOOKS.COM

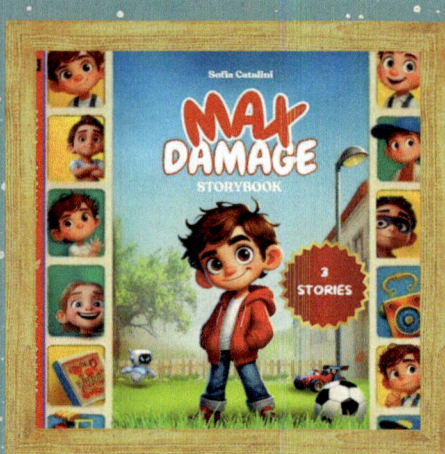

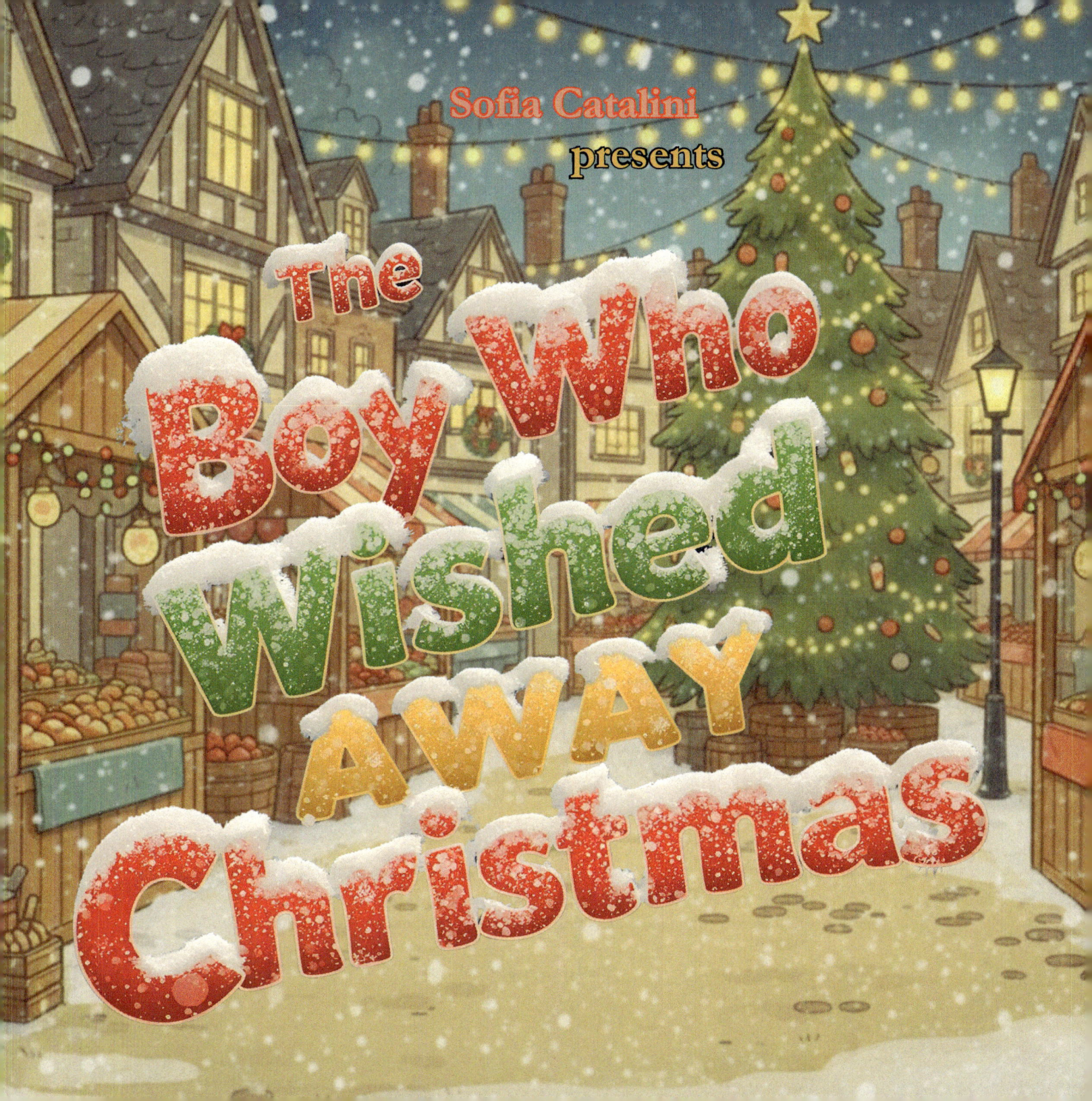

Dedicated to my wonderful children,
Christos, Alexandra and Eva

Copyright © 2025 by Sofia Catalini (IGESCA BOOKS)

All rights reserved. No part of this book may be reproduced, distributed
or transmitted in any form or by any mean, including photocopying, recording,
or other digital methods without the prior written permission of the author.
For permission requests, write to the author or visit the website address for details:

www.igescabooks.com

Disclaimer:
This is a work of fiction. Names, characters, places, events and incidents are
either the products of the author's imagination or used in a fictitious manner.
Any resemblance to actual persons, living or dead, or actual events is purely coincidental.

ISBN: 9798266977617

Gabriel was a bright ten-year-old boy.
He had once loved school,
loved solving puzzles
and loved to laugh with his friends.

But since last Christmas,
when his mother had died,
the world had felt unbearable,
like a dark cloud that never lifted.
His father tried his best.
His teachers and friends were kind.
But Gabriel's heart ached as the
25th of December drew closer.

One week before Christmas,
he sat on his bed unable to sleep,
staring at the photograph of his mother
that stood by his lamp.

Her smile was so beautiful and lively
in the picture that for a moment he
could almost believe she would walk
through the door again.
Then the truth struck him like ice:
She wouldn't.
Not this Christmas.
Not ever.
His mother's favourite holiday
had now become his worst nightmare.

Tears filled his eyes.

He got up and walked over to his window
and looked up at the midnight sky.
He focused on the brightest star.

Raising his hand, he seemed
to reach out to it.

"I wish Christmas would disappear,"
he whispered.
"What's the point of it anyway?"

The next morning, something was strange.
The Christmas tree in the living room
had vanished and his father had already
left for work, which was unusual.

On his way to school he saw Mrs. Finn,
his eighty-year-old neighbour looking sad.
She used to come alive at Christmas.
She would bake trays of biscuits
and hang garlands on her porch,
waiting for her children and grandchildren
to visit from London.
Now she sat slumped in her rocking chair,
staring into nothing, her house dark and silent.

Gabriel noticed that the streets were bare.
No glowing reindeer.
No fairy lights.
No tinsel.

Shops looked plain, their windows
empty of glitter and sparkle.

The Town Square, which was usually bursting
with stalls, laughter and music, lay bare too.
No market.
No cheer.
No lights.

At school, there were no smiles,
no decorations, no holiday songs being
sung from Mrs. Grady's music class.

The children dragged their feet,
tired and grumpy.

His friends acted indifferent,
sometimes even sharp with him.

At first, Gabriel felt surprised
and almost relieved.

Good, he thought. *No fuss, no fake happiness.
Just an ordinary day.*

But things at school got worse
when he was told there were no holidays;
not even a break on the twenty-fifth
or thirty-first of December.

Instead, there would be a maths test
on both those days. School suddenly
seemed lonelier and the world felt colder.

As days passed, he noticed how sad
and frustrated everyone seemed.

Even the local church had gone quiet.

The choir stalls were empty.

No voices rose into the night.

No church bells rang.

Nothing.

Bit by bit, Gabriel began to realise that it wasn't just Christmas he had wished away,
Birthdays had gone.
Easter too.
Valentine's, New Year's and every holiday that gave people joy.

It was as though he had stolen not only the decorations and parties but people's hope, kindness and love.
Even his father grew sharp-voiced and distant, as though all the warmth had been drained from him.

He began to feel hollow inside.

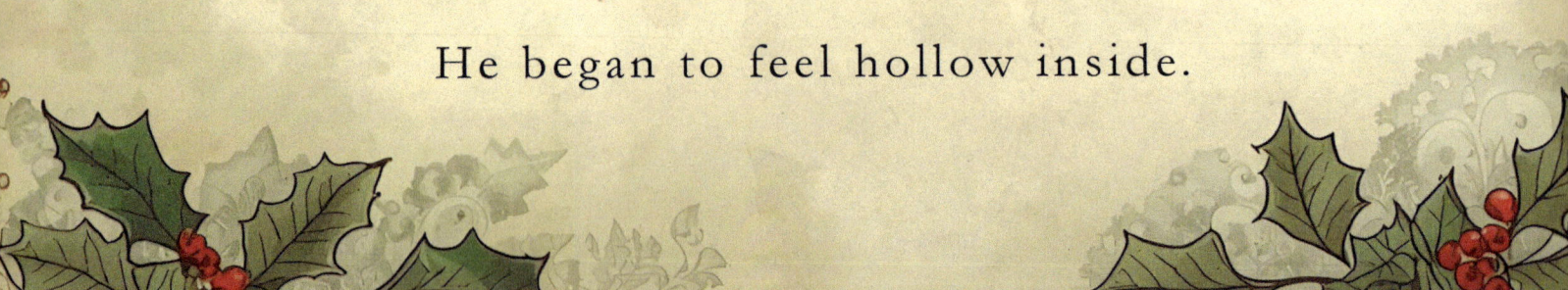

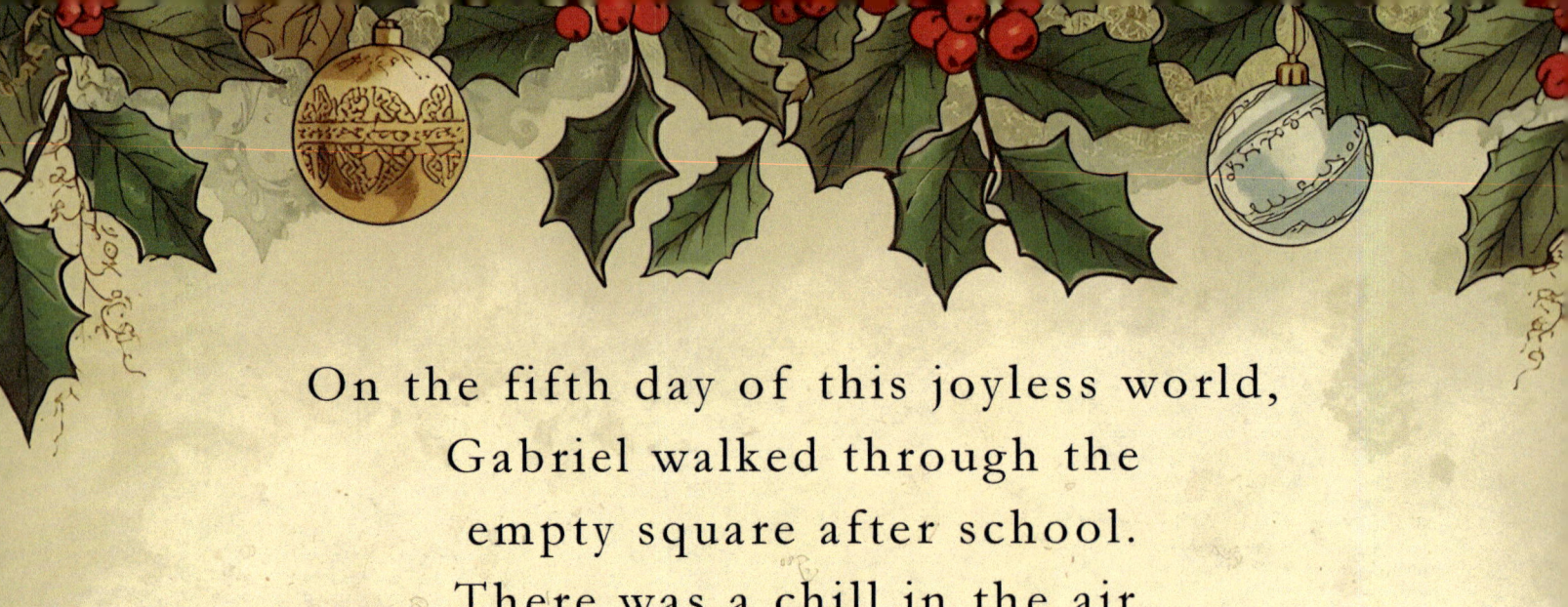

On the fifth day of this joyless world,
Gabriel walked through the
empty square after school.
There was a chill in the air.

Then he saw him:
an elderly man sitting alone on a bench.
His beard was white but unkempt.

His red velvet jacket worn thin
and filled with patches.
His black trousers were torn.
He thought he looked like a
poor man who had nowhere to go.

There was something odd about him.

Unlike everyone else, he was smiling.

His eyes, the clearest blue Gabriel
had ever seen, twinkled with something
that felt both kind and wise.

Drawn by curiosity, Gabriel walked
towards the bench and sat beside him.

"You look troubled,"
the elderly man said gently,
as though he had been waiting.

Gabriel sighed.

Normally, he wouldn't have talked to
a stranger but nothing about the
last few days seemed normal.

He looked at the man and mumbled,
"It's just... everything feels wrong.
Everyone's miserable.
There's no Christmas, no joy."

"Oh?" said the man curiously.

Gabriel lowered his head,
overwhelmed with guilt.
"I thought it was what I wanted.
I wished it all away."

"Wishes are a strange thing, you know,"
the man said, nodding slowly.

Gabriel tilted his head,
studying him with curiosity.

"What we think we want
may not be what we really need,"
he continued.
"Holidays aren't about gifts.
They're about bringing people together.
Take away the celebrations
and you risk taking away the
reason for people to smile at all."

Gabriel frowned,
feeling worse than before,
"But Christmas hurts me.
It reminds me that Mum isn't here."

"Of course it hurts,"
the man said kindly.
"Loss always does.
But love doesn't vanish
with the person we've lost.
Sometimes love is the very thing
that keeps us going.
Sometimes it is the greatest gift
they leave us."

The boy blinked at him.
"You sound like a teacher."

The man chuckled.
"I've been called many things...
never that."

His voice softened.
"Did you know your mother
once gave me a gift?"

Gabriel looked up sharply.
"Wha—what?
Did you know my mum?"

"Ohhh...I've known your mum
since she was a child,"
he replied.

"A long time ago, she lent me
something quite important
and wanted me to return it
when the time was right."

He glanced at Gabriel warmly,

"I may just give it you...
perhaps on Christmas Eve."

"But Christmas doesn't exist anymore,"
Gabriel whispered, looking down at his shoes.

The man only smiled, eyes twinkling.

"Sometimes all it takes
is to believe again—one wish,
made from love
instead of sorrow.

Do you *'believe'* Gabriel?"

Before Gabriel could say another word,
the man got up and disappeared
into the crowd that had suddenly
appeared in the square.

*How did he know my name? He wondered,
and where did all these people come from?
I could've sworn there was no one around.*

The next day was the 24th December and after
a long day at school, Gabriel was tired.

Once he arrived home, he went straight to
his bedroom and plopped down on his bed
thinking about the elderly man's words.

He remembered Mrs. Finn
sitting sadly on her porch,
his father's distant eyes,
the cold square without laughter,
and his mother's smile.

He had let grief turn him bitter.
He had wished away not just Christmas
but everyone's joy too.

With tears rolling down his cheeks,
he whispered:

*"I wish Christmas back.
I wish for love and for hope
and for Mum's memory
to make me... strong...not weak."*

Exhausted, he took a nap.

When he awoke, the world had changed.
From his bedroom window, he could see
fairy lights twinkling on the neighbourhood
houses and wreaths on doors.

He rushed downstairs and froze on the stairs,
looking out over the living room.
There it was again—their Christmas tree.
And under it lay a small wrapped parcel
with his name on it.
His father stood staring at it in astonishment.

"I didn't put that there,"
he said, bewildered.

With trembling fingers,
Gabriel unwrapped the parcel.

Inside was a wooden heart pendant
on a black string and an envelope.

He opened the letter.
It was from his mother.

Dear Father Christmas,

My name is Rosie and I'm 10 but I think you already know that.
My friends say you don't exist but I don't believe them because Nanna told me you're real!

A few months ago, Nanna went to heaven and I miss her so much.
I don't want a toy or anything like that; what I really want is for you to give my Nanna a kiss from me and my sister.
Tell her we're okay and that we love her a lot!
She believed in you very much so I know you will grant my wish.
You're magic, so I know you can do it.

I promise I will always share the spirit of Christmas and never forget you. I am lending you my lucky charm that I made with Nanna, to help give you strength while you deliver all the presents around the world.
Please return it to me when you think it's the right time.

Thank you,

Rosie Anderson

Gabriel's eyes blurred with tears.
He couldn't believe he was holding a
letter his mother had written...
to Father Christmas no less.

He could feel her presence and
was overcome with emotion.

As his hands trembled, he clutched his mother's
lucky charm. He turned the small wooden heart
over and saw words carved into its back:

"A heart carved by love will never be broken."

His father knelt beside him
and pulled him into a hug,
tighter than ever before.

For the first time in a year, Gabriel felt an
indescribable warmth, like an invisible blanket
of love which had mysteriously wrapped
around him—a reminder of how much he is loved.

From their living-room window, he noticed
a man across the street watching them.

The elderly man from the town square was
standing calmly under the street lamp.
His red jacket seemed larger and brighter,
sparkling softly in the darkness.
He smiled at Gabriel from a distance.
The night seemed to be enchanted,
with a gentle snowfall adding
a magical effect through the air.
Gabriel tilted his head and stared at him
through the window in unexpected awe.

"Father Christmas," he whispered.

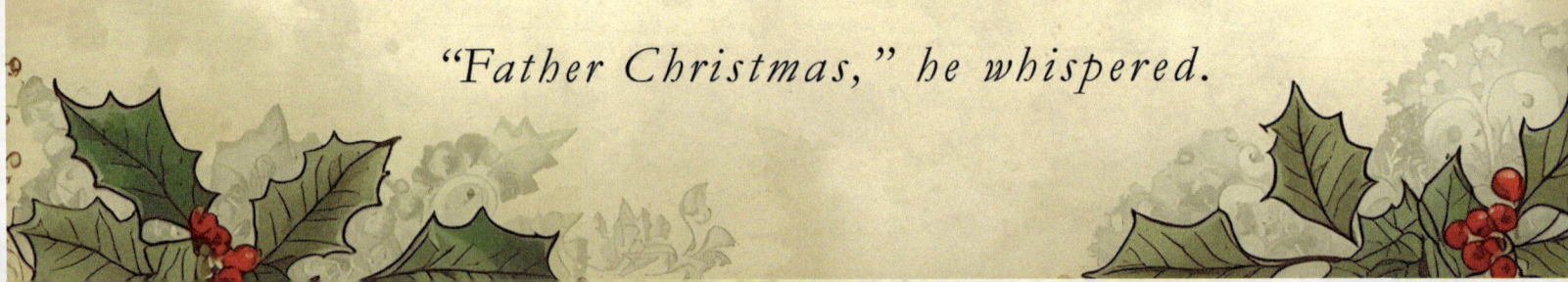

He rushed to the front door and opened
it quickly but there was no one there.
Father Christmas had vanished.

"What's the matter, Gabriel?"
asked his father in a sudden panic.

"Nothing, Dad. I thought I saw a friend."
He grinned.

He was sure he had seen him standing there.
How is any of this possible? he wondered.

He decided to be grateful and accept
the Christmas magic and smiled,
"Thank you."

He closed the door and looked at his
father who was still staring at him with
a worried expression on his face,
unsure of what had just happened.

"Can we go to the square dad?
I'd love a mince pie!"
chuckled Gabriel, suddenly feeling hungry.

"That sounds great! Let's go!"
answered his father happily.

As they grabbed their jackets and
stepped outside, they noticed a black cab
pulling up to Mrs. Finn's house next door.
She stood on the porch,
smiling broadly as it drew closer.
Two adults and three screaming children
jumped out of the taxi and ran towards her.

"Grandmaaaaa!" they cried.

Mrs. Finn's arms were already open wide
as she welcomed her grandchildren.

Yes, thought Gabriel, this is how it should be.

As they walked towards the square just
down the road, they could see it glowing
with stalls and crowded with families.

The neighbourhood houses were
decorated with twinkling lights.
The air was filled with
music, laughter and the
smell of roasted chestnuts.

Sadness had been replaced with happiness.
The joyous festivities had returned.

Finally arriving at the square,
he heard his friends shouting his name;
they were waving the mince pies
in their hands.

Gabriel smiled.

Things were back to normal.

A little later, as he wandered past the stalls,
he remembered slipping his mother's wooden
necklace into his jacket pocket.

He reached in and pulled it out.
For a moment, he looked at it, smiled,
and then placed it around his neck.

His father watched him lovingly.

He walked over to Gabriel and held his hand.

"Mum would be very proud of you son."
He smiled,
"Just like I am."

Gabriel blushed.

The thought of his mum and dad being
proud of him made him happy.

"Thanks dad. You're the best father in the world."
Smiled Gabriel, giving him a big warm hug.

His father, feeling a rush of emotions,
cleared his throat,
"Now go have some mince pie with your friends."

As Gabriel walked towards his friends,
he noticed a red glow
flashing across the sky.

"Whooaa!"

He immediately knew what it was and grinned.

"Thank you, Father Christmas."

He had finally understood why Christmas had always been his mother's favourite holiday:

It wasn't about the presents or the glitter.

It was about family and friends.

It was about love.

He touched the wooden heart around his neck once more and whispered his final wish of the year.

"Merry Christmas, Mum."

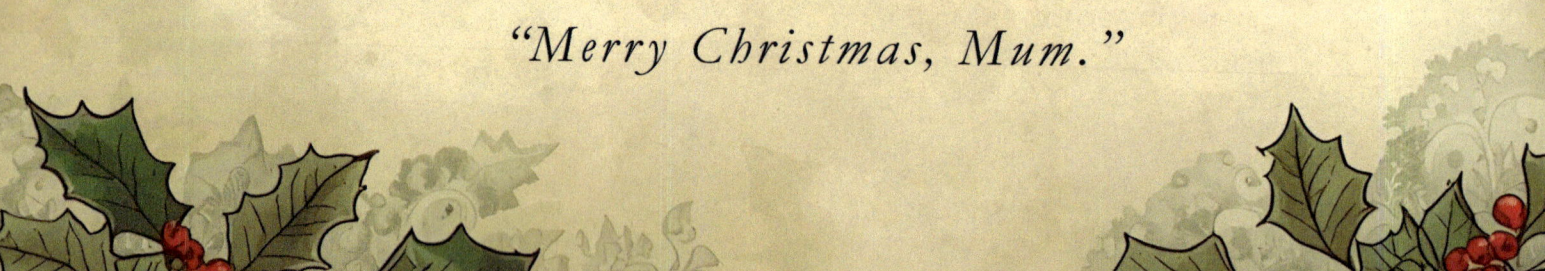

Write your letter to Santa

Your Opinion Matters.
Review Us Here.

Printed in Dunstable, United Kingdom